Queen Elizabeth I

Dorothy Turner

Illustrations by Martin Salisbury

The Bookwright Press
New York · 1987

Great Lives

Beethoven
Louis Braille
Captain Cook
Marie Curie
Einstein
Queen Elizabeth I
Queen Elizabeth II
Anne Frank
Gandhi
Helen Keller

John F. Kennedy
Martin Luther King, Jr.
John Lennon
Ferdinand Magellan
Karl Marx
Napoleon
Florence Nightingale
Elvis Presley
William Shakespeare
Mother Teresa

First published in 1987 by
Wayland (Publishers) Limited
61 Western Road, Hove
East Sussex BN3 1JD, England

First published in the
United States in 1987 by
The Bookwright Press
387 Park Avenue South
New York, NY 10016

ISBN 0–531–18132–4

Library of Congress Catalog Card Number: 87–
70039

Phototypeset by Kalligraphics Ltd, Redhill, Surrey
Printed in Italy by G. Canale & C.S.p.A., Turin

Contents

A royal birth

During the summer of 1533, King Henry VIII and his second wife, Anne Boleyn, eagerly awaited the birth of their child. The king was in a particularly good temper, for he believed that, at last, he was about to be given what he wanted – a son who could be heir to the throne. When Anne became pregnant, Henry consulted doctors, astrologers and witches, and they all agreed: the baby would be a boy.

Henry had waited a long time for a son. He had been married to his first wife, Katherine of Aragon, for more than twenty years. She had given him a daughter (Mary, now age seventeen) but she had failed to give him a son and was now too old to do so. So Henry defied the Pope, broke away from the Catholic Church, and divorced her. Then he married Anne.

At last, on September 7, Anne's baby was born at Greenwich Palace. To the intense

disappointment of her parents, and no doubt the dismay of those who had predicted otherwise, it was a girl. She was given the name Elizabeth, but her father was too distressed to attend the christening.

The baby princess was taken away to be brought up by servants in one of the king's fine houses in the countryside around London. She rarely saw her parents. She had little enough chance to see her mother; by the time Elizabeth was three, her father had had Anne Boleyn's head cut off.

So begins the extraordinary story of Elizabeth Tudor, who was to become Queen Elizabeth I, one of the greatest and best-loved of England's monarchs. But before becoming queen she had to suffer twenty-five years of intrigue and uncertainty.

A lonely childhood

After Elizabeth's birth, the king was still determined to have a son. Believing that he must have angered God by marrying Anne Boleyn, he began to look around for another wife. But first he had to get rid of Anne. She was accused of being unfaithful to Henry. When she was tried and found guilty the king ordered her head to be cut off, and the heads of those who were said to be her lovers. Anne was taken to the Tower of London and executed. The next day Henry married Jane Seymour.

Elizabeth, who was not yet three, was declared illegitimate. The title of princess was removed from her, some of her servants were dismissed, and the amount of money granted to her was cut. The woman in charge of her care soon had to write to the king begging for money for new clothes for the child: "She hath neither gown . . . nor petticoat, nor no manner of linen nor smocks . . ."

When Elizabeth was four, Henry's new wife, Jane Seymour, gave birth to a boy, called Edward. At last the king had the longed-for son. Elizabeth attended his christening, wearing a fine dress with a long train. Jane Seymour, however, died shortly after her son's birth.

The two motherless children, Elizabeth and Edward, spent

Anne Boleyn always claimed she was innocent.

6

much of their childhood together. Sometimes they were joined by their half-sister Mary, who was already in her twenties. Edward and Elizabeth were particularly close and wrote each other affectionate letters when they were separated. Apart from her governess, Katherine Ashley, Elizabeth had no one else to feel close to. She usually met her father only on state occasions. The king, now beginning to grow grossly fat, must have been an overwhelming figure to his two small children.

Elizabeth and Edward were close friends.

"The brightest star"

Elizabeth grew up to be clever and lively. In appearance she was tall and striking with long red-gold hair. She was energetic, with a powerful personality that attracted people to her, although some found her a little stiff and proud at times.

Like all of Henry's children she received an excellent education. At first she was taught by Katherine Ashley. Later she had a series of tutors from Cambridge who were among the most learned scholars of their day.

With her brother Edward,

Elizabeth had a good education and worked hard at her studies. Her language abilities helped her greatly when she became queen.

Elizabeth learned to read and translate Greek and Latin literature. In later life she astonished people by her ability to express herself fluently in Latin. She also learned French and Italian and was a fine speechmaker.

Religion was a very important subject of study. Elizabeth was brought up to be a Protestant, but she soon discovered that she disliked debate about the finer points of belief. She was never fanatical about religion, a fact that was later to help her when she ruled a religiously-divided England.

There is no doubt she was a gifted pupil. One of her tutors, Roger Ascham, said that he had known many well-educated ladies "but among them all the brightest star is my illustrious Lady Elizabeth."

Meanwhile, King Henry married three more times, but had no more children. His last wife, Catherine Parr, was an intelligent, educated woman. She took over the care of the king's children and, as Elizabeth's fourth stepmother, took the young girl to live with her at Chelsea.

Catherine Parr married Henry VIII in 1543.

and Queen Mary

...nuary,
...eth, who was
...d Edward were
...ther's death, they
clu... ...ch other and wept
bitter... In accordance with
Henry's will, Edward was to
succeed his father as king. Mary,
and then Elizabeth, were next in

line to the throne after him. In
fact, all three of Henry's children
were to rule England in turn.

After Henry's death nine year-
old Edward was crowned King
Edward VI, although various
powerful men actually governed
the country for him. The
temptation for ambitious

*The Lord Protector was the real
power behind Edward's throne.*

Queen Mary with her husband, Philip II of Spain.

courtiers to seize power was strong, and the young king's reign was full of political intrigue.

His reign lasted only six years. Edward was intelligent and learned, but he was not physically strong. He developed tuberculosis and, in 1553, died slowly and painfully at the early age of fifteen.

More intrigue followed. After various unsuccessful plots by ambitious families, Elizabeth's half-sister was crowned Queen Mary. The English had often had sympathy with "poor Mary," as she was sometimes called, for she had been pushed aside by Henry when he had divorced her mother, Katherine of Aragon. But there was one aspect of the new queen that many feared: she was an ardent Roman Catholic. Many Protestants were afraid she would try to bring Catholicism back as the official religion. Plots were soon hatched to replace her with her Protestant half-sister, Elizabeth.

A dark and fearful time

The plots to overthrow Queen Mary put Elizabeth in grave danger. Even if Elizabeth was innocent, people would think she was involved in treason. Eventually, the worst happened: Mary suspected her of being involved in a plot. Elizabeth was taken to the Tower of London and locked up in a small room. This was a dark and fearful time for her, and she was afraid she would be beheaded in the Tower, as her mother had been.

Fortunately Elizabeth was courageous as well as intelligent, and she defended herself well. Nothing could be proved against her. Instead, she was banished to

Mary had Elizabeth imprisoned in the Tower of London.

Protestants who refused to conform to Catholicism were executed.

Woodstock, near Oxford, and confined to a few miserable, drafty rooms in a crumbling mansion.

Meanwhile Mary further enraged people by marrying the heir to the Spanish throne – Prince Philip. Spain was a Catholic country and England's enemy.

Now it was Mary and Philip's turn to pray for a son. At last it was announced that Mary was pregnant. When the time came for the birth, everyone gathered at court eagerly. The time came and went, but no baby was born. It seems that Mary, desperate for a child, had only imagined that she was pregnant. Mary was

bitterly disappointed. Philip departed from England, leaving behind his aging, childless wife.

The last years of Mary's reign were marked by the cruel persecution of Protestants that earned her the nickname "Bloody Mary." Hundreds of people were burned alive.

Elizabeth was now twenty-two. She was allowed to return from imprisonment at Woodstock. Soon she settled herself and her servants at Hatfield House, outside London, where an unofficial court built up around her. As Mary began to show signs of fatal illness, all of Protestant England looked to Elizabeth to be their new queen.

Queen Elizabeth

Mary died on November 17, 1558. Elizabeth, next in line to the throne, was proclaimed queen of England the same day, amid great rejoicing.

Two months later, on January 15, 1559, Elizabeth – seated in a golden litter and wearing a dress so woven with gold that it was as stiff as armor – was carried in procession through London to her coronation. Crowds of excited people lined the streets, trumpets sounded and wine flowed freely. Elizabeth made a speech to the crowd, promising them she would be "as good unto you as ever queen was to her people." It was the beginning of an emotional relationship between monarch and subjects that was to last for many years.

Queen Elizabeth now faced the daunting task of bringing peace and prosperity to a country ruined by years of political turmoil. "I never saw . . . England weaker in strength, men, money and riches . . ." wrote a scholar at

the time.

The queen's first move was to put together a strong and effective government. She herself would rule the country, aided by a group of advisers. Fortunately she was an excellent judge of character. As chief adviser she chose Sir William Cecil (later called Lord Burghley). Cecil, a wise and experienced lawyer and diplomat, was to serve her, and England, outstandingly well for the next forty years.

As for Parliament, this had little of its modern power. The queen could call and dismiss it as she wished, and she could veto any bill she disliked. In all her long reign she held only a few Parliaments.

The queen's coronation was a day of great celebration.

The religious problem

The most urgent problem facing Elizabeth was the division between Catholics and Protestants, which could so easily lead to civil war. During Edward's reign England had become steadily more Protestant;

Elizabeth was not strongly religious and hated extremists.

during Mary's the country had swung back to Catholicism.

Elizabeth herself was not strongly religious, indeed it is difficult to know just what her views were. During Mary's reign she had professed to be Catholic and despite her Protestant upbringing had attended Mass.

As queen she at once had Parliament confirm that she was head of the English Church, as her father had been. (Before Henry's time, of course, the Pope in Rome had been head of the Church.) She also brought back King Edward's 1552 Prayer Book, with a few changes designed to please Catholics. To attend the Catholic Mass, however, became a crime punishable by imprisonment.

Disliking extremism of all kinds, Elizabeth and Cecil attempted a path of caution and compromise. Where the State seemed in danger, however, people were still put to death for their views, although in the forty-four years of her reign Elizabeth had fewer people executed than Queen Mary had had in just two years.

Religious differences did not go away, though. Radical Puritans

Queen Elizabeth holding one of her few Parliaments.

on the one hand and ardent Catholics on the other all became dissatisfied with Elizabeth's attitude to religion. Yet her policy did allow England a period of peace during which the country could gather its strength.

The rival queen

There were those who thought Elizabeth had no right to be queen. Some argued that Mary Stuart, Queen of Scotland and a grandchild of Henry VII, had a better claim to the throne. Mary was also a Catholic and there were many who wished to see England return to "the old religion."

Mary Stuart had been brought up in France and had married the French king. On his death she had returned to Scotland, remarried twice (both times unwisely) and been involved in scandal and murder. She so enraged the Scots that they rose against her in civil war. In 1568 Mary abdicated in favor of her son, James, and fled to England.

For almost twenty years she remained in England, a prisoner in various castles and country houses. The two queens, Mary and Elizabeth, exchanged portraits but never met.

Throughout all her years in England, Mary was a threat to

Elizabeth and Mary exchanged portraits but never met.

Elizabeth. Just as Elizabeth had been a focus for Protestants during her sister's reign, so Mary, Queen of Scots, gathered Catholic supporters around her during Elizabeth's. Mary's links with France made her especially dangerous. To Parliament and to Elizabeth's advisers, Mary was "a monstrous and huge dragon" that threatened the peace of England. But Elizabeth hesitated to have her own kinswoman, and a queen, executed. Nor would she release her from imprisonment.

At last, however, a decision had to be made. Mary was accused of treason, tried and found guilty. "For mine own life", wrote Elizabeth, "I would not touch her." But on February 1, 1587, she reluctantly signed Mary's death warrant. Mary was executed a week later.

Mary was executed in the great hall of Fotheringhay Castle.

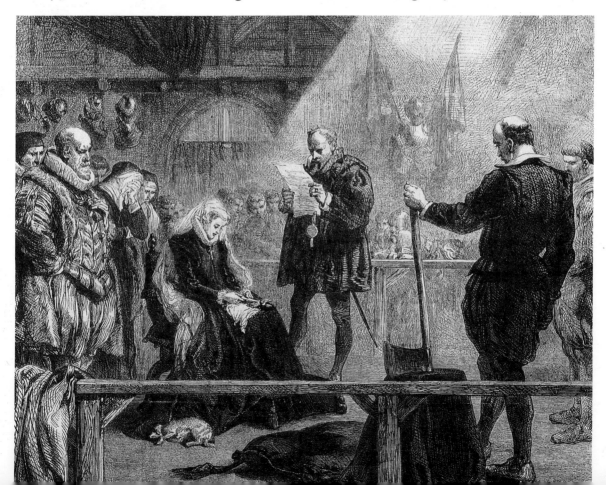

War with Spain

Elizabeth was not by nature warlike. In her own words, she wished for "a peaceable, quiet, and well-ordered state and kingdom." During the 1580s, however, the international situation worsened. Philip II, the powerful king of Spain (who had once been husband to Queen Mary) decided that England should be returned to Catholicism. To do this he would have to overthrow Elizabeth, "that guilty woman of England," as he called her.

In 1588 England stood in great danger as Philip planned his invasion. Compared to the great European powers of France and Spain, England was a small, weak country.

The Spanish planned to sail up

the English Channel from Portugal, meet up with Spanish troops in the Netherlands and from there invade England. In the early summer of 1588 an Armada of 130 ships, carrying 20,000 soldiers, set off through the Channel toward the Netherlands.

Meanwhile an English army gathered at Tilbury, on the banks of the Thames, preparing to defend the country. Queen Elizabeth herself addressed the troops. In a famous speech she promised "to live or die among you all . . . I know I have the body of a weak and feeble woman, but I have the heart and stomach of a king."

The Spanish invasion failed. The skill and daring of the English captains, with their more maneuverable and better-armed English ships, defeated the Armada. Some Spanish ships were sunk; some were blown by gales into the North Sea. Many were wrecked on the long journey back to Spain. The Spanish threat was overcome. It was the high point of Elizabeth's reign.

The Spanish attack was not well planned, so England was victorious.

"A very great princess"

Elizabeth took care of her appearance.

The queen, at the height of her powers, was a formidable figure who dominated the courtiers and politicians that clustered around her. As a Spanish visitor to her Court remarked: "She had her way absolutely as her father did."

She was also clever, stubborn, determined and highstrung. Her moods were fast-changing, even dangerous when she was angry, for she could be very violent and cruel at times.

Despite being surrounded by endlessly feasting courtiers, Elizabeth ate little and always remained thin, angular and sometimes ungainly. She loved activity. The tall, pale-skinned and red-haired figure of the queen could often be seen riding fast horses in the hunt or dancing energetically with her courtiers. In quieter moments she enjoyed playing music, watching actors and listening to poetry.

Elizabeth loved fine clothes and jewels and endlessly fussed over her appearance. Much of her life was spent in ill health,

however, and a nearly fatal attack of smallpox left her face scarred.

Queen Elizabeth was a complex, mysterious figure. Even those close to her felt they did not know her, for she was highly skilled at concealing her true feelings and quite capable of lying and deceit if it suited her. Perhaps the lonely years of her childhood had taught her that there were few people, if any, whom she could trust.

To her subjects, however, she was more than all these things. She was Gloriana, the Virgin Queen, the mighty Elizabeth who, in the words of a French ambassador, was "a very great princess who knows everything."

Elizabeth enjoyed dancing. Her only problem was finding partners able to keep up with her.

The marriage problem

François Hercule de Valois, Duke of Aleçon.

Why did she never marry? This is the most intriguing unanswered question about Queen Elizabeth. Everyone wanted her to marry. In those days it was considered unnatural for a woman to rule at all, and for a queen to remain unmarried was even more disturbing. Also, it was vital for her to have an heir.

Despite her many suitors, Elizabeth never married. It is clear from the way she treated him that she was in love for many years with Robert Dudley, whom she made Earl of Leicester. There were other favorites at court after Leicester. There was also no shortage of suitors from the royal families of Europe. When she was forty-five she almost married the French king's twenty-four-year-old brother, the Duke of Alençon. She seemed as infatuated by her "frog" (as she affectionately called him) as she had been years before by Leicester, but the marriage never took place. She seemed sincere, but no one could ever fathom her real feelings.

Throughout her reign rumors circulated about her private life. The rumors marred her reputation, but still she would not marry.

Perhaps memories of her mother's fate colored her views. It is probable, too, that Elizabeth was unwilling to relinquish her power and authority to a man, as she would have to if she married. Once, when Leicester quarreled with her, she reprimanded him with the words: "I will have but one mistress and no master," that is, she would make her own decisions and would submit to no man's will. And she would never discuss who should be her heir.

Elizabeth was a strong-willed, self-reliant woman.

Elizabeth's England

We look back to Elizabeth's long reign as a period of great vitality. As the new ideas of the Renaissance and Reformation brought fresh energy to England, the forty years of relative peace enabled the country's scholars, scientists, artists and explorers to flourish.

The first of Shakespeare's plays were performed in Elizabeth's reign. Some of them

Drake presented plundered gold and jewels to the queen.

were put on privately at the queen's court, but even the humblest of her subjects could see performances at the newly built public theaters in London, as well as plays by many other fine dramatists. Music, poetry and architecture also flourished, and every educated person learned to sing, play an instrument, dance and write verse.

At this time, too, England's influence began to spread around the world, as explorers traveled to new lands. Walter Raleigh sailed to North America, where he set up the short-lived colony of Virginia, named after the Virgin Queen. Francis Drake sailed around the world, bringing back plundered gold and precious jewels. Exploration led to trade and the foundation of England's future prosperity.

Not everyone shared in this prosperity, however. Most of the population of England and Wales still lived and worked in the countryside. Although conditions

The poor did not really benefit from England's prosperity.

for the growing middle classes improved, life was still desperately hard for the poor.

But it is for its achievements that this period of history is largely remembered. Elizabeth became the glorious symbol of all the glittering success of her age. Unlike any other Tudor monarch, she gave her name to a whole era – the Elizabethan age.

The end of an era

At the turn of the century, the golden sun of Elizabeth's England seemed to dim. There were serious outbreaks of plague; bad weather led to poor harvests and hunger; the people began to feel the effect of heavy taxes and rising inflation. Repressive measures against Catholics and Puritans became stronger. Even the queen's personal popularity began to fade.

William Cecil and Leicester were both dead. In their places were Robert Cecil (William's son) and the Earl of Essex (Leicester's godson). These two were rivals,

James I of England in his ceremonial robes.

until Essex's rising against the queen led to his execution.

Elizabeth withdrew from the world. Sad and listless, she grew increasingly short-tempered and given to bouts of weeping. During her final illness she ate nothing and hardly uttered a word. Not one of her close companions was left.

The problem remained – who would be her successor? Despite repeated demands from Parliament, Elizabeth refused to discuss the subject. Now, during her illness, her councilors arranged for King James VI of Scotland (son of Mary, Queen of Scots) to inherit the throne.

Early on March 24, 1603, the queen died in her sleep at Richmond Palace, at the age of sixty-nine. When her death was announced there was "great weeping and lamentation among the lords and ladies." At once a horseman was dispatched to the north to inform James that he was now King James I of England.

Elizabeth's death ended one of the most famous eras in history.

Important dates

1533   Elizabeth born, September 7.

1536   Anne Boleyn, Elizabeth's mother, beheaded.

1537   Edward VI born.

1547   Henry VIII dies. Edward VI comes to the throne.

1553   Edward VI dies. Mary I comes to the throne.

1554   Elizabeth imprisoned in the Tower of London. Mary marries Philip II of Spain.

1558   Mary I dies. Elizabeth I is proclaimed queen, November 17.

1559   Coronation of Elizabeth I, January 15.

1568   Mary, Queen of Scots, flees to England.

1587   Mary, Queen of Scots, executed.

1588   The Spanish Armada defeated. Death of the Earl of Leicester.

1598   Death of William Cecil (Lord Burghley).

1601   Essex's rebellion and execution.

1603   Death of Queen Elizabeth, March 24. James VI of Scotland becomes James I of England.

Glossary

Abdicate   To resign, especially to give up the throne of a country.

Armada   A fleet of armed ships.

Catholic   Belonging to the Roman Catholic Church, headed by the Pope.

Church of England   The Protestant Church in England, set up by Henry VIII when he broke away from the Pope.

Heir to the throne   The person who is next in line to inherit the throne of a country.

Illegitimate   Illegal; born of parents not legally married.

Litter   A couch carried by bearers.

Monarch   A king or queen.

Protestant   Belonging to one of the churches that broke away from the Catholic Church in the Reformation of the sixteenth century.

Puritan   An extreme Protestant who opposed the Church of England and wished to set up a simpler form of worship and a strict moral code.

Reformation   The movement that led Protestant churches to break away from Catholicism.

Renaissance   The rebirth of classical learning and culture that took place in Europe from the fourteenth to the sixteenth centuries.

Stuart   Surname of the Scottish family that ruled England after the Tudors. James VI of Scotland (James I of England) was England's first Stuart king.

Treason   Plotting to betray or overthrow a government or ruler.

Tudor   Surname of the Welsh family that governed England from 1485–1603. Henry VII, Henry VIII, Edward VI, Mary I and Elizabeth I were all Tudors.

Veto   To forbid or reject something.

Books to read

Elizabeth I and Tudor England by Stephan White-Thompson. Franklin Watts, 1985.

Elizabethan Court by Marjorie Reeves. Longman, 1978.

Growing Up in Elizabethan Times by Amanda Clarke. David & Charles, 1980.

Kings and Queens of England by L. Dugarde Peach. Merry Thoughts, 1968.

Queen Elizabeth I by Betka Zamoyska. McGraw, 1981.

Queen Elizabeth, The Queen Mother by Alan Hamilton. David & Charles, 1984.

Seven Sovereign Queens by Geoffrey Trease. Vanguard, 1969.

Tales from English History: For Children by Agnes Strickland. Richard West, 1978.

Women Who Changed History: Five Famous Queens by Mary L. Davis. Lerner, 1978.

Index